Minnesota Activity Book

by Paula Ellis, illustrations by Shane Nitzsche

To Lake Superior, my home away from home.

~Paula

Cover design by Jonathan Norberg
Book design by Lora Westberg

10 9 8 7 6 5 4 3 2 1

Copyright 2013 by Paula Ellis
Published by Adventure Publications, Inc.
820 Cleveland Street South
Cambridge, MN 55008
1-800-678-7006
www.adventurepublications.net
All rights reserved
Printed in U.S.A.

ISBN: 978-1-59193-377-9

Welcome to Minnesota

The land we call Minnesota was once covered by giant glaciers. As the glaciers melted, the landscape was formed. From northeastern Minnesota's Eagle Mountain (the highest point in the state) to the flat prairies in the southwest, glaciers left hills, valleys, rivers—and thousands of lakes. Minnesota is nicknamed the Land of 10,000 Lakes for a reason!

Eventually, the first Native Americans came to the area. By the 1600s, European explorers arrived. They met the Ojibwe and Dakota Indians that lived there. The land was full of natural riches, so others followed to this place of opportunity. Fur traders, including French-Canadians called Voyageurs, came in their canoes. They traded tools, blankets and other goods with the Native Americans. Loggers soon began chopping down trees from the thick forests, and miners came searching for gold and other valuable metals. Pioneers in covered wagons rode in to farm the land, and fishermen settled along the shores of Lake Superior.

Minnesota became the 32nd state of the United States on May 11, 1858. The state took its name from the Minnesota River, which came from two Dakota Indian words: "minni" and "sotah." Together, the words mean "sky-tinted water."

Life wasn't easy for the early settlers. Short summers and extreme winters made it hard to live off the land. Grasshoppers ate the farmers' crops, and forest fires destroyed countless trees. Blizzards blew across the land, and wars with Native Americans created great danger for people.

Those difficult times made Minnesota strong. Today Minnesotans are hard-working people. Plus, with the state's many parks and recreational areas, the people of Minnesota play hard, too. Minnesotans enjoy activities such as biking, canoeing, hiking, skiing, fishing, snowmobiling and camping.

What do you want to do in Minnesota?

- ☐ catch a fish
- ☐ go canoeing
- ☐ listen to loons
- ☐ see an ore boat
- ☐ find an agate
- ☐ play in the snow
- ☐ shop at the Mall
- ☐ cross the Mississippi
- ☐ watch a hockey game

Minnesota Map

Use the map to find the answers.

What country is on the northern border of Minnesota?

☐ Mexico   ☐ France   ☐ Canada   ☐ Norway

How many states border Minnesota? (hint: Canada is not a state)

☐ 1   ☐ 2   ☐ 4   ☐ 6   ☐ 7

Circle the names of the states that border Minnesota:

Wyoming	Illinois	Kansas	Hawaii	Alaska	California
North Dakota	Wisconsin	Colorado	Oklahoma	New York	Iowa
Montana	Nebraska	South Dakota	Missouri	Florida	Ohio

(answers on page 62)

Minnesota State Symbols

State Flag

State Bird Common Loon

State Flower Showy Lady's Slipper

State Gemstone Lake Superior Agate

State Butterfly Monarch

State Fish Walleye

State Tree Red or Norway Pine

State Fruit Honeycrisp Apple

State Grain Wild Rice

Minnesota Fun Facts

Minnesota is called the Land of 10,000 Lakes, but there are actually more than 15,000 lakes throughout the state.

Minnesota has more shoreline than California, Florida and Hawaii combined.

Minnesota reaches farther north than any other US state, except Alaska.

Minnesota's coldest recorded temperate came on February 2, 1996. In the town of Tower, the air temperature fell to 60 degrees below zero.

There's more water in Lake Superior than in the rest of the Great Lakes put together: Lake Michigan, Lake Huron, Lake Erie and Lake Ontario.

Minnesota's Mall of America Field (also known as the Metrodome) is the only stadium in the world to host all of the following: a Super Bowl, NCAA Final Four basketball game, Major League Baseball All-Star Game and the World Series.

The first successful open heart surgery was performed at the University of Minnesota in 1952.

In Minneapolis, there are eight miles of skyway walkways, allowing people to walk from building to building without going outside. It's the largest connected skyway system in the world.

Saint Paul is Minnesota's capital city. But before the town became known as Saint Paul, it was called Pig's Eye.

In 1922, Ralph Samuelson invented waterskiing on Lake Pepin in southeastern Minnesota. He was just 18 years old.

Minnesota's largest known walleye ever caught weighed almost 18 pounds and was about 36 inches long. It was snagged in the Seagull River, which flows into Saganaga Lake, the deepest natural lake in the state.

Tonka toy trucks were first made in Minnesota.

In Red Wing, you can see the world's largest leather boot. It's 20 feet long, 16 feet high and 7 feet wide. It's a size 638½.

Francis Johnson spent 29 years rolling a ball of twine. Now found in Darwin, it weighs about nine tons and is called the world's largest twine ball rolled by one man.

ABCs of Minnesota

Take a trip through the alphabet in the State of Minnesota.

A is for **Arrowhead**, northeastern Minnesota's shape and nickname

B is for **Buttons**, made in the early 1900s from Lake Pepin clam shells

C is for **Curling**, a sport played on ice with a stone and brooms

D is for **Dwarf Trout Lily**, a wildflower that's only found in Minnesota

E is for **Eveleth**, home of the US Hockey Hall of Fame

F is for **Fishing**, enjoyed by many in the Land of 10,000 Lakes

G is for **Grand Portage**, where furs were once traded for food & supplies

H is for **Honeycrisp**, a popular type of apple first grown in Minnesota

I is for **International Falls**, so cold that it's called the Icebox of the Nation

J is for **Jolly Green Giant**, the mascot of Green Giant vegetables

K is for **Kellogg**, hometown of the popular LARK Toy Store

L is for **Lynx**, Minnesota's professional women's basketball team

M is for **Mosquito**, a pesky insect that some jokingly call the State Bird

N is for **North American Bear Center**, where people learn about bears

O is for **Scott Olson**, a hockey player who invented Rollerblades

P is for **Pillsbury**, a Minnesota company that makes baking ingredients

Q is for **Quarry Park**, where granite stone was cut from the ground

R is for **Red River**, which borders parts of Minnesota and North Dakota

S is for **Skijoring**, skiing while being pulled by a horse, snowmobile or dog

T is for **Twine Ball**, a famous attraction found in the town of Darwin

U is for **Up North**, where many people go for a weekend away

V is for **Vikings**, early explorers from Northern Europe

W is for **Wheaties**, a breakfast cereal first eaten in Minneapolis

X is for **X-rays**, which doctors use at the Mayo Clinic in Rochester

Y is for **You Betcha**, a Minnesota phrase that means "yes"

Z is for **Zamboni**, a machine that smooths the ice at hockey games

Mall of America

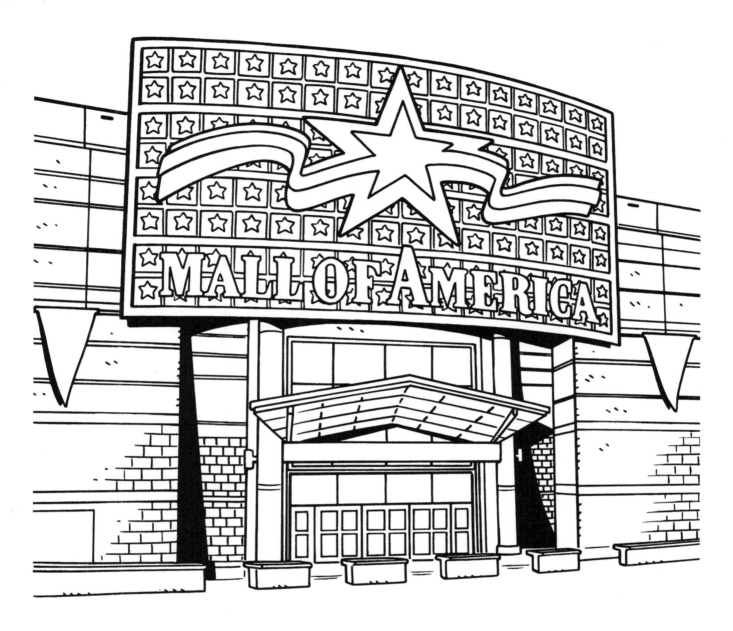

Where can you go shopping, attend a wedding, watch a movie, play with LEGO toys, ride a roller coaster and see sharks—all under one roof? The Mall of America! Located in Bloomington, the Mall is so big that it would take almost four days to spend just 10 minutes inside each of the Mall's more than 520 stores!

The Mall of America is very popular. Each year, more people visit there than Disney World!

Native Americans

Dakota (Dah-ko-tah) and Ojibwe (Oh-jib-way) are Native American tribes. They were enemies and fought over the land of Minnesota. The tribes hunted, fished and gathered wild rice. The Ojibwe are also known as Chippewa Indians. The Dakota were sometimes called Sioux, a cruel name which means "little snakes."

 Native Americans used to put leeches on sick people. They believed this would suck out the illness!

The Land of 10,000 Lakes

```
R  B  S  W  A  T  E  R  D  T  H  A
F  A  L  E  A  C  R  O  C  K  J  S
L  P  I  O  M  S  P  I  D  E  R  E
G  E  B  N  N  A  O  C  C  L  Z  P
K  L  E  E  Y  G  P  A  F  E  T  T
O  I  M  C  N  A  L  N  I  P  R  B
R  C  I  U  H  N  A  O  S  H  E  I
U  A  D  Q  D  A  R  E  H  A  B  F
D  N  J  U  G  G  L  E  R  N  E  X
P  V  I  S  L  A  N  D  W  T  I  H
H  I  A  W  A  T  H  A  G  L  L  E
B  C  E  Y  G  L  S  W  A  V  E  M
```

BEMIDJI	LEECH	RAINY
ELEPHANT	LONG	RICE
HIAWATHA	MUD	ROCK
ISLAND	PELICAN	SAGANAGA
JUGGLER	POPLAR	SPIDER

**Minnesota actually has more than 15,000 lakes.
Can you find the 15 lake names above?**

(answers on page 62)

Laura Ingalls Wilder

Laura Ingalls was a pioneer girl. Her family moved to Walnut Grove when she was seven years old. When she was older, she married a man named Almanzo Wilder. Laura wrote nine books about growing up and life on the prairie. Her books later inspired the creation of a popular television show called *Little House on the Prairie*.

Laura became a teacher when she was just 15. Her first book wasn't published until she was 65 years old!

Agate Hunting

More than a billion years ago, the land of northeastern Minnesota was covered in lava. As this lava cooled, it became rock. Water carried minerals into holes inside the rock. This formed a beautiful, new type of stone: Lake Superior Agate. Today, people go agate hunting to look for these colorful rocks!

 In the town of Moose Lake, trucks dump rocks on the street every July, so people can hunt for agates!

Gunflint Trail

The Gunflint Trail is a 57-mile road that begins in Grand Marais and ends at Saganaga Lake, on the Canadian border. People travel the Gunflint Trail into the wilderness of northeastern Minnesota. There, they go fishing, canoeing, camping, cross-country skiing and see wild animals such as moose, black bears and eagles.

 The Gunflint Trail gets its name from flint, a type of rock. Flint was used to help make old guns fire!

Park Rules

Camping in Minnesota's state parks and recreation areas can be a great way to spend your vacation. The parks were made for us to enjoy, with opportunities for swimming, hiking, marshmallow roasting and sleeping under the stars. Remember to respect other campers, the park and the animals.

Rules help to keep everyone safe. Circle the things above that are not safe or are against the rules.

(answers on page 62)

Twin Cities

Saint Paul is the capital of Minnesota. The city across the Mississippi River is Minneapolis. Together they are called the Twin Cities. They are the largest cities in the state. The Twin Cities are known for their beautiful lakes and parks, and as places that value art and theater.

The Twin Cities are among the best places in the USA for _____. Connect the dots to find out what.

(answer on page 62)

Jeffers Petroglyphs

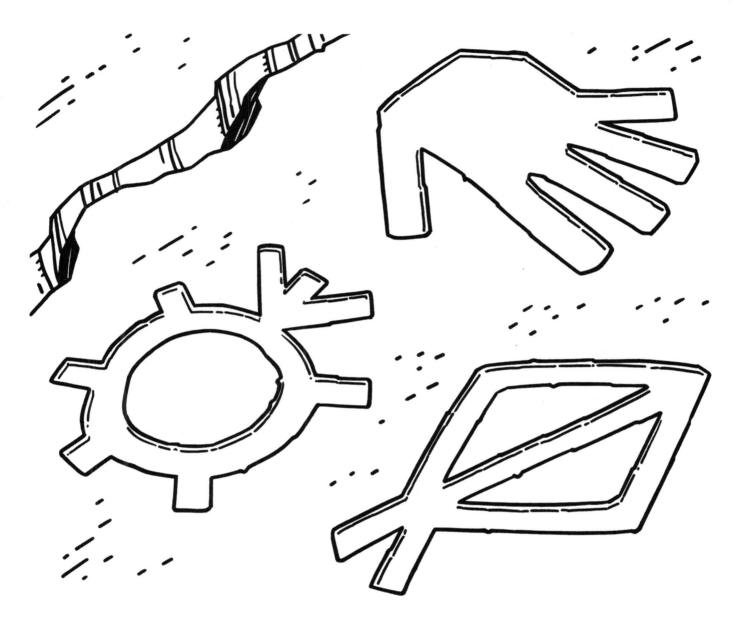

About 10,000 years ago, American Indians came to the area of south-western Minnesota. They created petroglyphs, or pictures carved into rocks. Outside the small town of Jeffers, ancient petroglyphs can still be found. No one knows for sure what the pictures and symbols mean.

 What do you think the symbols above look like? Make up a story that includes the things that you see.

Winter Fun

Across

3. An outdoorsman's lake home
5. A cold person's cry
7. For cross-country or downhill
8. Water does this in the cold
9. Ten degrees, for example
11. Minnesota's official state sport

Down

1. Famous dogsled driver
2. Travel over snow on a snow___
3. He'll be back again some day
4. No two are exactly alike
6. They keep your hands warm
10. It clears snowy roads

Minnesota winters can be cold but lots of fun. Fill in the crossword puzzle, and learn more about winter.

(answers on page 62)

Showy Lady's Slipper

The Minnesota State Flower is the Showy Lady's Slipper. It is pink and white, and it gets its name because it looks like a woman's shoe. The beautiful wildflower is found in swamps and woods. Lady's Slippers grow very slowly and usually don't flower until they're about 15 years old.

 Never pick Lady's Slippers because the plants will die. If they aren't picked, they can live up to 100 years!

John Beargrease

Long before a road was built on the North Shore of Lake Superior, there was a young Ojibwe Indian from Beaver Bay named John Beargrease. John and his brothers carried mail by boat and dogsled to the villages between Two Harbors and Grand Marais. John's fastest trip was about 90 miles in 28 hours by dogsled.

 The John Beargrease Sled Dog Race celebrates John's important life with a race along the North Shore!

Minnesota State Fair

The Minnesota State Fair began in 1859, just a year after Minnesota became a US state. Also called the Great Minnesota Get-together, the fair is famous for its food on a stick. Try everything from spaghetti and meatballs and pizza to s'mores and candy bars—all served on a stick. What do you think would taste good on a stick?

 The Minnesota State Fair's average daily attendance makes it the largest state fair in the United States!

Boundary Waters Canoe Area

The Boundary Waters Canoe Area Wilderness, or BWCAW, is along the Canadian border in northeastern Minnesota. Thousands of years ago, glaciers helped to carve the landscape of this region, which is home to more than 1,000 lakes. People visit the BWCAW to canoe, camp, fish, hike and explore the lakes and trails.

Canoeists portage (carry) their canoes from lake to lake. Help the canoeist portage through the maze above.

(answer on page 62)

Paul Bunyan

Paul Bunyan and his blue ox, Babe, are make-believe characters. There are many tall tales about Paul, a giant man known as the king of all lumberjacks. In one story, Paul's footsteps made all of the lakes in Minnesota. Another said that the buttons on his baby shirt were wagon wheels.

Paul Bunyan is so popular that there are 26 statues of him throughout the state of Minnesota!

Sigurd Olson

The wilderness is a special place. Wildlife, clear blue lakes and thick forests are worth protecting for future generations to see. Sigurd Olson was a man who worked to protect the environment. He was a writer who worked to help people understand how important the wilderness is to our future.

You can take care of the wilderness by picking up trash. What other ways can you help? Write down your ideas.

Split Rock Lighthouse

Split Rock Lighthouse was opened in 1910. Its light warned passing ships of the dangerous rocks near the North Shore of Lake Superior. In 1969, thanks to technology such as radar, the lighthouse was no longer needed. Now it only shines on November 10, the day the *Edmund Fitzgerald* sank in 1975.

You could hear the lighthouse's horn from five miles away and see its light from over twenty miles away!

Scandinavians

Scandinavians are people mostly from the countries of Norway, Denmark and Sweden. Many Scandinavians live in Minnesota, bringing Scandinavian traditions with them. Foods like lefse, lutefisk and Swedish meatballs are favorite dishes eaten by Scandinavians in Minnesota.

 Ole & Lena are silly Scandinavian characters. Can you tell which picture above is different than the rest?

(answer on page 62)

Iron Range

The Iron Range is located in northeastern Minnesota. It is one of the best places in the world to find iron ore, which is used to make steel. The ore is dug out of rock and sent by train to Lake Superior. There, ships carry the ore to mills to be made into steel for cars, buildings and other products.

 The *Edmund Fitzgerald* was a ship that carried iron ore across Lake Superior. In 1975, it sank in a terrible storm!

Famous Minnesotans

Hubert __ __ __ __ __ __ __ __ ran for president in 1968.
      8 21 13 16 8 18 5 25

Charles __ __ __ __ __ __ __ created Charlie Brown and Snoopy.
       19 3 8 21 12 20 26

Ann __ __ __ __ __ __ __ __ reached the North and South Poles.
    2 1 14 3 18 15 6 20

Bob __ __ __ __ __ is a famous singer and songwriter.
    4 25 12 1 14

Justine __ __ __ __ __ __ __ was a Boundary Waters guide.
       11 5 18 6 15 15 20

Will __ __ __ __ __ __ crossed Antarctica by dogsled.
    19 20 5 7 5 18

James J. __ __ __ __ built the Great Northern Railway.
         8 9 12 12

Roger __ __ __ __ __ hit home runs for the New York Yankees.
     13 1 18 9 19

Jesse __ __ __ __ __ __ __ was a pro wrestler and governor.
     22 5 14 20 21 18 1

Garrison __ __ __ __ __ __ __ is a great storyteller and writer.
        11 5 9 12 12 15 18

Jesse __ __ __ __ __ tried to rob a bank in Northfield.
     10 1 13 5 19

Mary __ __ __ __ __ __ __ __ created the Harry Potter covers.
     7 18 1 14 4 16 18 5

A	B	C	D	E	F	G	H	I	J	K	L	M	N	O	P	Q	R	S	T	U	V	W	X	Y	Z
1	2	3	4	5	6	7	8	9	10	11	12	13	14	15	16	17	18	19	20	21	22	23	24	25	26

Many famous and important people have come from Minnesota. Use the code to identify the people above.

(answers on page 62)

Common Loon

The Common Loon is the state bird of Minnesota. Loons have red eyes that can see underwater to find fish to eat. Most birds have hollow bones that help them fly, but loons' bones are solid. This makes them heavier and allows them to dive more than 200 feet deep. Loons can stay underwater for almost five minutes at a time.

Loons cannot take off from land. In order to fly, they have to start in a body of water, such as a pond or a lake!

Made in Minnesota

```
W  S  P  U  H  T  E  N  K  A  N  R
A  P  S  N  O  W  M  O  B  I  L  E
T  A  Z  P  C  A  N  D  Y  B  A  R
E  M  A  S  K  I  N  G  T  A  P  E
R  O  L  L  E  R  B  L  A  D  E  S
S  H  B  V  Y  M  C  B  M  J  P  B
K  A  J  U  S  W  U  E  E  K  I  U
I  Y  D  R  T  K  I  K  R  N  Z  S
S  D  T  M  I  T  T  N  L  E  Z  E
J  E  O  W  C  B  O  O  D  U  A  S
D  N  Y  Y  K  G  S  N  Y  O  K  L
S  T  A  P  L  E  R  H  S  S  W  S
```

BUS
BUTTON
CANDY BAR
CEREAL
HOCKEY STICK

MASKING TAPE
MUKLUKS
PIZZA
ROLLERBLADES
SNOWMOBILE

SPAM
STAPLER
TOYS
WATER SKI
WINDOWS

**Many things have been invented and made in Minnesota.
Can you find the listed ones in the puzzle above?**

(answers on page 63)

Target Field

Target Field is a baseball park in Minneapolis and is the home field of the Minnesota Twins. The stadium has about 40,000 seats for fans to watch their favorite players. The scoreboard is bigger than over a thousand TVs. After Sunday games, kids get to go out on the field and run the bases.

Target Field isn't just for baseball. Some couples rent the field in order to get married at home plate!

Gopher

Two similar types of gophers live underground in Minnesota: the Plains Pocket Gopher and the Northern Pocket Gopher. The gophers use their sharp front claws and large front teeth to dig tunnels. The gophers are named for the pouches, or pockets, in their cheeks, where they store food to eat later.

Both types of gophers appear to be almost the same. Connect the dots above to see what they look like.

Ice Fishing

Minnesota winters are so cold that lakes freeze on top, and ice fishing is a favorite activity. Fishermen drill or chop holes in the ice, and they fish through the holes. Many fishermen take small houses called fish houses onto the lake. They keep warm inside the fish houses while fishing through the floor!

Some fish houses are really fancy. They are heated and have beds, kitchens and even television sets inside!

Lake Itasca

Lake Itasca is located in north central Minnesota. The lake is famous because it is where the Mississippi River begins. Water from Lake Itasca flows down the middle of the USA to the Gulf of Mexico. Take off your shoes at Itasca State Park, and walk across the Mighty Mississippi where it's just a few feet wide.

 The historical sign at the start of the river says 2,552 miles. But the river is now about 2,300 miles long.

Dorothy Molter

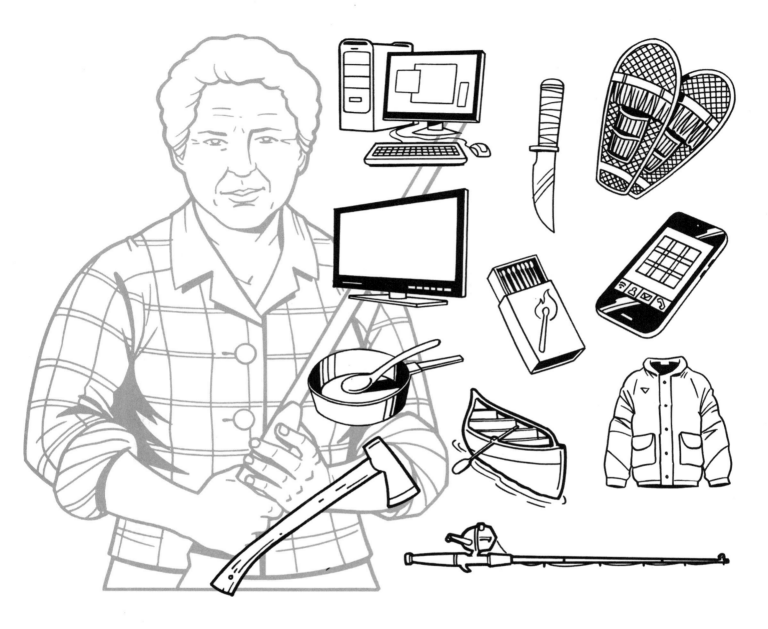

Dorothy Molter lived alone in the Boundary Waters Canoe Area Wilderness with no electricity or running water. Her home was 15 miles from the nearest road, but she had many visitors. She enjoyed making homemade root beer for those who passed by, and she became known as "the Root Beer Lady."

Dorothy fished and hunted for some of her food. Circle the items that you think she used to survive?

(answers on page 62)

Harvest Time

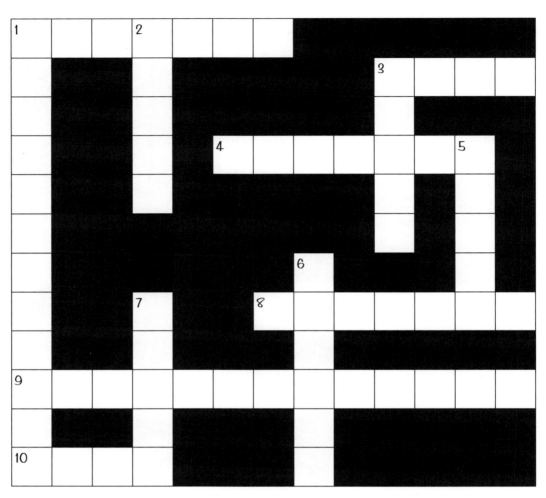

Across

1. Machine that's used to harvest grain
3. Some "farm" this when it blows
4. Thanksgiving's not their favorite holiday
8. A field for cows
9. It comes from a brown cow?
10. A house for farm animals

Down

1. This veggie is a July 4th favorite
2. Soy__ are used to make cooking oil
3. Flour is made from this
5. __beets become a sweet ingredient
6. Where beef comes from
7. Pigs provide this breakfast meat

Farming is important in Minnesota. Use the clues above to fill in the farming-themed crossword puzzle.

(answers on page 63)

International Wolf Center

The International Wolf Center, in Ely, teaches people about the lives of wolves. At the visitor center, there are educational programs and special exhibits. Children can participate in games and activities, and guests of all ages can watch real wolves as they play together and develop hunting skills that help them survive.

 When wolf pups are born, they are blind and deaf, and they only weigh about one pound!

Lake of the Woods

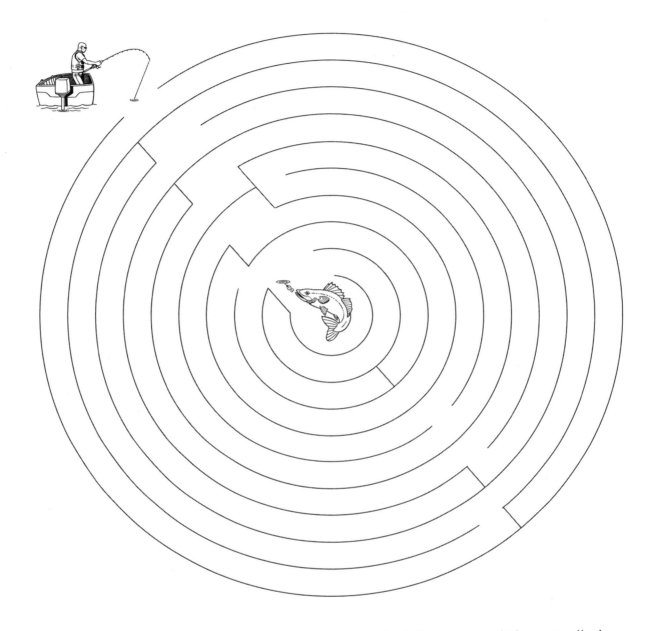

Lake of the Woods is the most northern lake in Minnesota. It is actually in two countries: the USA and Canada! The Northwest Angle is land that sticks out into Lake of the Woods from Canada, but the land belongs to Minnesota. Some fishermen believe Lake of the Woods has the best fishing in the world.

Help the Lake of the Woods fisherman find his way through the maze to catch a big walleye.

Charles Lindbergh

Charles Lindbergh grew up near Little Falls. In May of 1927, he flew his plane, *The Spirit of St. Louis*, from New York to Paris, France. He became the first person to fly alone, without stopping, across the Atlantic Ocean. It took him almost 34 hours. Today, the flight takes less than eight hours.

A big gas tank blocked his view, so Charles had to look out an open side window during his whole flight!

Fill in the Blanks

```
            __  M  __ __ __ __ __
                I  __ __ __ __ __
        __ __ __ __  N  __ __
      __ __ __ __ __ __  N  __ __
    __ __ __ __ __ __ __  E  __
          __ __ __  S  __
        __ __ __ __ __  O  __ __
          __ __ __  T  __ __
      __ __ __ __ __  A  __ __
```

1. Mall of _____.

2. Lake where the Mississippi River begins.

3. Explorers who came to the land of Minnesota from northern Europe.

4. Tall tales say that his footprints made the Great Lakes.

5. Minnesota's state sport.

6. This animal's name means "twig eater."

7. Famous lighthouse that warned ships of rocks along the Lake Superior shore.

8. Valuable Lake Superior gemstones that people look for in Minnesota.

9. The capital of Minnesota.

(answers on page 63)

Kensington Runestone

In 1898, a young boy found a 200-pound stone in a field near the town of Alexandria. The Kensington Runestone, as it came to be known, had writing on it that showed it was left there by Viking explorers. It led some people to believe that the Vikings—and not Columbus—"discovered" America.

Some still believe in the Kensington Runestone, but many people think it's fake—a trick or a joke!

Winter Carnival

The Winter Carnival in Saint Paul is called "the coolest celebration on earth."
People come to see snow carvings, a parade and even an ice palace. A
popular event is the hunt for the carnival medallion, or coin. People collect
clues to be the first to find the medallion, hidden somewhere in the city.

 **Search above. How many carnival medallions
can you find hidden somewhere in the picture?**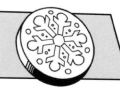

(answers on page 63)

Judy Garland Museum

At the Judy Garland Museum in Grand Rapids, you can learn all about one of the town's most famous people, Frances Ethel Gumm. Frances began singing at 2½ years old. When she was 12, she changed her name to Judy Garland. At age 16, she played the role of Dorothy in the famous movie *The Wizard of Oz*.

Judy's childhood home is part of the museum. Help the family through the maze, so they can tour the house!

(answer on page 63)

State Parks

```
T  K  G  J  A  Y  C  O  O  K  E  P
M  L  R  O  L  D  M  I  L  L  J  I
L  Z  A  C  R  O  W  W  I  N  G  C
M  I  N  N  E  O  P  A  T  J  N  N
A  P  D  S  C  S  C  F  T  E  A  I
P  P  P  T  P  A  I  A  I  S  T  C
L  E  O  C  A  I  R  B  M  S  U  S
E  L  R  R  R  F  T  L  L  D  R  C
W  B  T  O  K  D  T  A  E  E  E  E
O  A  A  I  F  U  N  O  S  Y  Y  N
O  Y  G  X  C  A  M  P  N  C  B  I
D  N  E  F  R  O  N  T  E  N  A  C
```

AFTON	GRAND PORTAGE	OLD MILL
CAMDEN	ITASCA	SIBLEY
CARLEY	JAY COOKE	SCENIC
CROW WING	MAPLEWOOD	ST CROIX
FRONTENAC	MINNEOPA	ZIPPEL BAY

People enjoy hiking, biking and fishing in Minnesota's state parks. Can you find the state parks listed above?

(answers on page 63)

Valleyfair

Valleyfair Amusement Park in Shakopee has everything. If you think your swingset is fun, try the Xtreme Swing. Forty people at once can ride it. On a hot summer day, take a dip in the wave pool at Soak City waterpark. Screams, roller coasters and even deep fried pickles are waiting for you. Have fun!

Every October, Valleyfair transforms into one of the state's spookiest haunted attractions: ValleySCARE!

Voyageurs National Park

Voyageurs National Park, near the Canadian border, is the only national park in Minnesota. It was named after the traders called Voyageurs who paddled their canoes across lakes and rivers during the 1600s, 1700s and 1800s. Today, you might see people traveling the national park's waters by houseboat.

 The park has some of the oldest rocks in the world. Some still have scrapes left by moving glaciers!

Walleye

The walleye is the state fish of Minnesota. It is named for its large, cloudy eyes. A covering, or "wall," over its eyes helps it to see better at night and to prey upon smaller fish. The walleye is a favorite fish to eat in Minnesota. Fishermen across the state catch about three-and-a-half million walleyes each year.

The largest walleye caught in Minnesota weighed almost 18 pounds! Connect the dots to reel in your own walleye.

Fort Snelling

Historic Fort Snelling stands upon the bluff where the Mississippi and Minnesota Rivers come together, south of the Twin Cities. Long ago, Native Americans came to the fort to trade furs. People traveling west stopped for supplies and rest. Soldiers trained there, and today people come to learn about Minnesota's history.

Visitors can see what life was like 200 years ago, march with the soldiers and even help to load a cannon!

Wild Rice

Wild rice is special to Native Americans, who consider it "a gift from the creator." It grows in lakes and rivers in many parts of the state. To harvest wild rice, people sometimes paddle canoes across the water and tap the stalks with sticks. This causes the wild rice to fall in order to be collected, dried, cooked and then eaten.

 Wild rice isn't really rice at all. It's a type of grass, and the "rice" that we eat is actually the grass's seeds!

Hockey

Minnesota is called the State of Hockey, and ice hockey is the state's official sport. When the lakes freeze, kids know it's time to play ice hockey. Some children learn to skate as soon as they learn to walk. Many grow up dreaming of scoring the winning shot for the Minnesota Wild.

 Hockey pucks are made of rubber. But some of the first hockey pucks were square and made of wood!

Gooseberry Falls

In northeastern Minnesota, the Gooseberry River flows toward Lake Superior. Five waterfalls together form Gooseberry Falls. The falls are the main attraction of Gooseberry Falls State Park. People visit the park to watch the rushing water as it crashes over the falls.

Millions of years ago, lava and glaciers helped to form the falls! See how at the visitor center's theater.

49

Minneapolis Sculpture Garden

What's a giant spoon with a cherry on top doing in a park? It's one of more than 40 pieces of art in the Minneapolis Sculpture Garden. The garden is among the largest sculpture gardens in our country. There's plenty of room to play, explore and have fun—and it's free.

The cherry on top of the spoon weighs 1,200 pounds. That's one big cherry! Find it through the maze above.

Alan Page

Alan Page was a star football player for the Minnesota Vikings. He also went to school to become a lawyer. Years after he retired from football, he became an important judge for the Minnesota Supreme Court in 1992. He was the first African American to be elected to a statewide office in Minnesota.

How good was Alan Page at football? Many consider him to be the best Vikings player ever!

Moose

The moose is the largest wild animal found in Minnesota. Moose only eat plants, and their name comes from the Native American word "mooswa," which means "twig eater." Moose have no upper front teeth; they use their lips to break twigs off trees and eat them. Moose also love eating plants that grow in water.

 Moose are big, but they're also fast. At only five days old, a baby moose can run faster than a person!

Pipestone National Monument ~

Pipestone National Monument is a historic area, sacred to the Plains Indians. A soft red stone is found here, and it is used by Native Americans to make pipes carved by hand. Native Americans believe smoke from these pipes carries their prayers to the Great Spirit.

The Pipestone area is so sacred that warring tribes are said to have stopped fighting when they went there!

Know Minnesota

Across

2. It begins at Lake Itasca
4. Minnesota's world-famous hospital
5. It's mined in northern Minnesota
8. A 57-mile road in the northeast
10. Lake Superior gemstones
11. Sacred rock used for pipes

Down

1. Split Rock is one
2. The largest wild animal in Minnesota
3. People portage it in the BWCAW
6. The state fish of Minnesota
7. Also known as Chippewa Indians
9. Bloomington's __ of America

Use the clues above to fill in the squares and learn more about the state of Minnesota.

(answers on page 64)

Duluth

Duluth is Minnesota's fourth-largest city. It is an important shipping port on Lake Superior and a popular place for tourists. In Duluth, visitors can do all sorts of different things: ski, golf, run in Grandma's Marathon, visit the Great Lakes Aquarium or even tour a real ore ship, the *William A. Irvin*.

 Duluth is "The Christmas City of the North." A big parade before Thanksgiving starts the Christmas season!

Minnesota Bingo

If you see one of the people, places, animals or objects on the bingo card, mark it with an X. Be sure to mark the free space in the middle. If you get five Xs in a row, you win! Remember to yell "Bingo!"

B	I	N	G	O
STATUE	COW	FREIGHTER	LIGHTHOUSE	BUTTERFLY
MALL	BOAT	ROLLER COASTER	CORN FIELD	TRACTOR
FISH	DEER	FREE	BARN	WIND TURBINE
TENT	BRIDGE	SILO	BASEBALL	SUNFLOWER
INTERSTATE SIGN	RIVER	EAGLE	PUBLIC ART	TRAIN

License plate game: Cross out letters as you see them.

A B C D E F G H I J K L M N O P Q R S T U V W X Y Z

Mayo Family

William Mayo came to Rochester from England. He was a doctor, and his two sons, William and Charles, also became doctors. The three of them started Rochester's Mayo Clinic. It has grown into a world-famous hospital. People come from all over to receive special care at the Mayo Clinic.

 William and Charles learned a lot by watching their father and helping him with his patients!

National Eagle Center

Countless Bald Eagles live along the Mississippi River in Minnesota. Eagles dive and skim the water to catch fish with their sharp talons. The National Eagle Center is located in the southeastern city of Wabasha. The Center studies eagles and takes care of injured birds. Visitors can meet the eagles that live at the Center.

 Bald Eagles aren't actually bald. The name may come from the old word "balde," which means white!

Quiz Your Parents

1. What was the capital city of Saint Paul formerly known as?

2. What does the name "Minnesota" mean?

3. What special name were the French-Canadian fur traders called?

4. Who wrote *Little House on the Prairie*?

5. What is the Minnesota state gemstone?

6. What best-selling kind of apple was first grown in Minnesota?

7. True or false? There are more than 1,000 stores in the Mall of America.

8. What nickname are Minneapolis and Saint Paul commonly known by?

9. What is the name of the state flower that looks like a woman's shoe?

10. What legendary character is known as the king of all lumberjacks?

11. What does BWCAW stand for?

12. What popular water sport was invented by a Minnesota teenager?

13. Who became famous for flying his plane across the Atlantic Ocean?

14. What was Frances Ethel Gumm's more famous name?

15. What fish is named for its large, cloudy eyes?

16. Wild rice isn't really rice. What is it?

17. What Hall of Fame football player became a state supreme court judge?

18. What is the largest wild animal in Minnesota?

19. Where does the Mississippi River begin?

20. What end-of-summer event is known for all of its food on a stick?

(answers on page 64)

59

Father Hennepin

Father Louis Hennepin came to America as a missionary in the 1670s. His jobs were to explore the New World and to spread his religion. He wrote about the area of Minnesota and the Mississippi River. Father Hennepin is credited with discovering and naming Minneapolis's Saint Anthony Falls.

Father Hennepin is important to Minnesota's history. An avenue, county and state park are named after him!

Name the Animals

1. _____

2. _____

3. _____

4. _____

5. _____

6. _____

7. _____

8. _____

Name the animals you might see in Minnesota.

(answers on page 63)

Answers

Page 3—Minnesota Map

1. Canada
2. Four
3. Iowa, North Dakota, South Dakota, Wisconsin

Page 9—Land of 10,000 Lakes

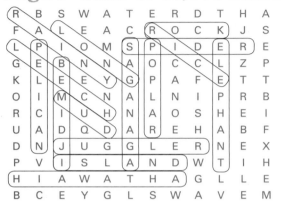

Page 13—Park Rules

ax in tree, dog off leash, garbage by tent, fire not watched, fire outside fire pit, swimming kids not watched, loud music, spilled drink not cleaned up

Page 14—Twin Cities

The Twin Cities are considered one of the best places in the USA for bicycling.

Page 16—Winter Fun

Page 20—Boundary Waters

Page 24—Scandinavians

Page 26—Famous Minnesotans

1. Hubert Humphrey
2. Charles Schultz
3. Ann Bancroft
4. Bob Dylan
5. Justine Kerfoot
6. Will Steger
7. James J. Hill
8. Roger Maris
9. Jesse Ventura
10. Garrison Keillor
11. Jesse James
12. Mary Grandpre

Page 33—Dorothy Molter

ax, canoe, coat, cooking pan, fishing pole, knife, matches, snowshoes